THE MARVEL SUPER HEROES GUIDE BOOK

BY MEGAN STINE

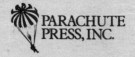

PARACHUTE
PRESS, INC.

Parachute Press, Inc.
156 Fifth Avenue
New York, NY 10010

Published by Parachute Press, Inc.

ISBN: 0-938753-56-8

First printing: September 1991

Printed in the U.S.A.

Design by Michel Design

CONTENTS

INTRODUCTION

WHAROOOM! POW! SCRUNNNNCH! FOOMP!
BLAM! BLAM! BLAM!

What's up? Is someone about to get creamed? Is the world going to explode?

Naaaah . . .

It's just an old comic book trick—a trick to get your attention and make you excited about what's happening on this page!

If you've ever read a comic book, you already know what those words mean. They're the special sounds and signals of heroes and villains in battle. BLAM! often means a criminal just fired a round of bullets at someone like Captain America or Wolverine. And SCRUNNNNCH! can mean that Spider-Man just slammed into a solid brick wall. And WHAROOM! usually means that something or someone exploded—the bigger the letters, the bigger the blast!

But do you really know all the secrets of the super heroes? Do you know how Daredevil got his powers—or his name? Or how Spider-Man's web-shooter works? Do you know who's in charge of the West Coast branch of the Avengers?

Well, fear no more. Because the answers to all of these questions—and MORE—are just a few pages away.

In this book you'll find out which super heroes are the strongest . . . which villains are the strongest . . . and who would win in a one-on-one test of strength! You'll read about the Baddest Bad Guys . . . and the Best Weapons. You'll find out which super heroes can be trusted to remain true to the fight against evil. And which ones have become traitors to the cause!

Best of all, you'll find out how each of your favorite super heroes got his or her super powers in the first place.

So turn the page, but watch out . . . BOOOOOOOOM! The facts about all the best super heroes are about to explode in THE MARVEL SUPER HEROES GUIDE BOOK!

FAMOUS FOREVER:
THE
GREATEST GOOD GUYS
IN MARVEL HISTORY

TM

Look out, Spidey! Here comes a 20-ton pile of bricks! It's going to fall on your head if your don't move FAST! And then you'll be smashed into a red and blue pile of crud.

But hey—who are we kidding? Everyone knows that Spider-Man is the first and last word in Marvel Super Heroes. He's the number-one good guy, the best. And he's been famous forever. So it's very unlikely that Spidey will ever get totally smashed or squished.

After Spider-Man, there are about five or six other super heroes who are also *almost* indestructible. They're the all-time best of the costumed crime-fighters—the ones with the most impressive powers and the most righteous sense of duty. Other heroes may have moments of weakness, but these guys never fail to save the world from evil.

So here's a brief look at the greatest good guys in Marvel history—including their "origin stories" telling how they got their powers in the first place. These are the guys you can pretty much count on to be around years from now.

Unless . . .

Look out, Spidey! Here comes a 50-megaton truckload of TNT!!

....

SPIDER-MAN

Spider-Man's real name is Peter Parker, and he was orphaned when his parents were killed in a plane crash. From then on, Peter lived with his aunt and uncle, May and Ben Parker, in a suburb of New York City. As a teenager, Peter was supersmart but shy, and didn't have many friends. One night, while attending a lecture and demonstration about radiation, Peter was bitten by a spider that had accidentally been zapped with radiation.

Instantly, Peter developed a number of superhuman powers. He found he had tremendous strength, great reflexes, and a superior sense of balance. He also discovered that he had the ability to make parts of his body—especially his hands and feet—stick to other surfaces. (That's how he can walk up walls like a spider.)

Soon Peter began using his powers in a public way. Wearing a mask and calling himself the Amazing Spider-Man, Peter appeared on a television show as a fantastic stuntman. At first he planned to use his powers only to become famous in show business. But after the television show one night, something happened that changed Peter's life. A burglar ran past him, and Peter didn't do anything to stop the man—even though he could have used his superpowers to stop him easily.

A few days later, this same burglar broke into Peter's house and murdered his uncle. Dressed as Spider-Man, Peter helped the police capture the burglar. But he was filled with grief and regret, knowing that if he had stopped the burglar himself, the tragedy might never have occurred.

At that moment, Peter Parker resolved to use his powers to fight crime.

In addition to his physical abilities, Spider-Man possesses one other, very important superhuman power. It's a form of ESP called his "spider-sense." When danger is near, Spidey gets a tingling sensation in the back of his skull. This "spider-sense" acts like a warning signal, giving him advance notice when someone is about to hit him or fire a gun at him. Together with his superlative reflexes, Spidey is almost always able to dodge the bullets that come his way.

Although Spidey can't fly, he manages to get around using his one and only weapon: his web-shooters. Peter Parker invented the web-shooters and now always wears them on his wrists. The web-shooters can be used in a million different ways. They can shoot a single thin strand of "web fluid," which is a superstrong substance, like a tough nylon cord. Spidey can swing from it, or use it to lower himself from tall buildings. The web-shooter can also produce a web or net which Spidey often uses to trap his victims.

Spider-Man is sometimes called the first modern superhero. He started his career in 1963. The 1960s were a time of change for this country. And Spider-Man was a real change from the heroes that came before him. Spidey has real human problems: job problems, girl problems. He gets confused. He questions things. Sometimes he doesn't like being a super hero at all. But lucky for his fans, he always sticks to it.

• •

CAPTAIN AMERICA

Captain America has been around for more than 50 years. He came on the scene in 1941—the same year the U.S. entered World War II. And he was the perfect hero for his time—brave, patriotic and 100% American! His real name is Steve Rogers, and he first appeared as a teenager determined to fight the Nazis. Steve Rogers, however, was a sickly teenager—not exactly Nazi-fighting material. But he was so sincere about wanting to join the Army that he was given an experimental Super-Soldier serum by the Army. The serum turned him into a perfect human specimen, and he was given the name Captain America. But the scientist who invented the serum was murdered shortly after administering it to Steve, so Steve is the only person ever to benefit from this amazing formula. Now Steve Rogers is as strong as any human can possibly be.

Although technically Captain America has no superhuman powers, he has more agility, speed, endurance, and better reflexes than any ordinary human on Earth, including Olympic athletes. He has also studied boxing and judo, and he exercises every day to stay in shape.

After World War II, Captain America disappeared for a while. (In fact, he plunged into the icy waters of the English Channel and remained there for decades in suspended animation.) But then he was revived by the Avengers and is now one of the most important members of that crime-fighting team.

His only weapon is a red, white, and blue shield, given to him by the U.S. government. It is made from a combination of two incredibly tough metals. (One of them is Adamantium, the same artificial metal that has been applied to Wolverine's skeleton.) Captain America's shield is the only one of its kind in the world, and it's virtually indestructible.

DAREDEVIL

Like the young Spider-Man, Matthew Murdock was a bit of an outcast in his youth. He was an excellent student but a scrawny weakling taunted and teased by other kids in school. The kids called him "Daredevil" as a way of mocking him, since they actually thought he wouldn't dare to do anything dangerous at all. So, secretly Matt began to work out and soon he was in great shape.

But one day, using his new athletic abilities, Matt threw himself in front of a truck in order to save the life of a blind man. The truck, however, was carrying radioactive waste materials and Matt got hit with a ton of radiation. The accident left him blind but also with superhuman senses in the areas of touch, hearing, taste, and smell. After a horrible episode in which Matt's father was murdered by criminals, Matt decided to use his powers to fight crime. Remembering the name with which he had been teased as a kid, Matt chose to call himself Daredevil and has been a costumed crime-fighter ever since.

Matt's senses are so well developed now that even though he is blind, he can easily tell the difference between identical twins at a distance of 20 feet—just from the tiny differences in smell! He can remember the scent of any person he's ever met, as long as he spent at least five minutes with that person. He can even follow people by locating their scent and following it through a crowd.

His super sense of hearing allows him to detect the presence of someone in a room—by listening to the person's heartbeats! Daredevil can also tell if people are lying from the sound of their heartbeat. And he can hear someone whispering in the next room, even through a soundproof wall. Loud sounds can be very painful to Daredevil, however—and he would probably go nuts at a rock concert.

With his super sense of touch, Daredevil is able to detect tiny changes in room temperature, so that even if his hearing and sense of smell are somehow blocked, he can still tell when someone enters a room by their body heat. Daredevil also has a kind of radar that allows him to feel or "see" objects. No one is sure how this radar works, but with it Daredevil is able to recognize objects, obstacles, and buildings almost as well as a sighted person could.

Daredevil's only weapon is a Billy Club—a portion of Matt Murdock's blind man's cane. He removes the crook of the cane and uses the straight shaft as a weighted stick in fights.

THOR

Thor is a warrior, an adventurer, and a Norse god who is prince of the world called Asgard. His father is Odin, the chief ruler of the gods of Asgard. His mother is Gaea, goddess of the Earth. Odin's idea, when he decided to have a son with Gaea, was that Thor should have both earthly and godly powers. Consequently, Thor divides his time between Earth and Asgard and feels at home in both worlds.

Thor has been around for a lon-n-n-n-ng time, so he has a lot of history—and a lot of problems. His biggest problem is that his adopted brother, Loki, hates him and wants to destroy him. So far, however, Loki has not succeeded and Thor is still the heir to the throne.

Throughout the years, Thor has spent much time on Earth with various identities. At one time, in fact, his father erased his memory and sent him to Earth as a crippled medical student to learn

14

humility. But lately, Thor calls himself Eric Masterson when on Earth.

As Eric Masterson, Thor wears modern clothes and possesses none of his powers. But when he stamps his walking cane on the ground, it changes into Thor's weapon, an enchanted hammer, and Eric is instantly transformed back into Thor.

Thor's hammer is named Mjolnir, and it is one of the coolest weapons around. For one thing, when Thor throws it, it always returns to his hand. For another, he uses it to fly by throwing it forward and grasping the handle. (See page 56 for more details.)

Best of all, Thor is immune to all earthly diseases and is one of the strongest super heroes alive. He has Class 100 strength, which means he can lift more than 100 tons. That's about 70 tons *more* than most other Asgardian gods can lift.

As if that's not enough to make Thor famous forever, he is also one of the founding members of the famous crime-fighting team, the Avengers.

WOLVERINE

To start with, we're talking about a guy who has real metal claws as part of his body. He has also had his skeleton laced with Adamantium, the strongest metal known to exist. So is it any wonder that Wolverine feels slightly inhuman from time to time? Is it a surprise that he has some wild tendencies? Tell the truth—would you feel like being a nice guy if you had sharp metal claws that were more than a foot long?

Wolverine's whole past is mysterious. For many years, not even Wolverine himself knew exactly how he became the strange superhuman that he is today. But here's as much of the story as is known.

James MacDonald Hudson, an official in a secret department of the Canadian government, was honeymooning with his wife, Heather, in Canada's Wood Buffalo National Park. While they were in the woods, Wolverine suddenly appeared and, behaving like an animal, savagely attacked them. (Wolverine's name was Logan at the time—just Logan. No one knows if that's his first name, last name, or what.)

Heather shot and wounded Logan, and then she and her husband took him to their cabin. There they comforted and nursed him until he began to act less like an insane animal and more like a human being. It was in this cabin, by the way, that Logan first saw his own claws.

When Logan calmed down, he announced that in addition to his claws, he also had had Adamantium bonded to his skeleton. The metal makes it nearly impossible for Logan's bones to be broken—but the shock of the Adamantium-bonding process is probably what turned Logan into a wild creature. Logan also has a superhuman healing ability that allows him to recover from almost all wounds. That's probably how he could undergo the Adamantium-bonding surgery in the first place, and still survive.

Years later, Logan learned that a secret criminal conclave had given him his claws.

Eventually Logan went to work for the Canadian government. For a time, he was the leader of Alpha Flight, a group of superhuman secret agents. His code name was Weapon X, but he was also sometimes called Wolverine. Now he is a member of the X-Men. Most of the time, Wolverine uses his powers to fight evil-doers. But once in a while, he still loses his temper and just goes berserk!

TM

WOLVERINE

BADDEST BAD GUYS

When it comes to villains, some of them are almost as indestructible as the *good* guys! No matter how many times Spider-Man faces the Kingpin, for instance, the Kingpin keeps coming back for more. The same is true about Thor's archenemy, Loki, who also happens to be Thor's adopted brother. No matter how politely Thor asks, Loki just won't go away.

In fact, just about every super hero has one or two enemies who really know how to hang in there. (And in Spider-Man's case, there are a lot more than two! But hey—what do you expect? Spidey can handle it.)

So here they are: the Baddest Bad Guys around.

It's hard to say which of these bad guys is the worst, most vile, most evil, most despicable villain ever to bring terror to the innocent people of Earth. Let's just say they're all winners in the "Not First Choice for Best Friend" category!

KINGPIN

The Kingpin is a big man—in every sense of the word. Physically, he's a 450-pound tub of *muscle*, not lard! He's also a big man in the world of crime. Not counting the Maggia (which is a collection of organized crime families), the Kingpin is the biggest and most important leader of crime gangs on the East Coast. Of course he tries to hide his illegal dealings behind his legitimate business operations. But he's not fooling anyone! The Kingpin's real name is Wilson Fisk, and through the years he's had to deal with both Spider-Man and Daredevil, his archenemies. At one point, Spider-Man came out of retirement to stop the Kingpin from totally taking over the crime scene in New York. Recently, however, Daredevil has been the Kingpin's biggest enemy.

But sometimes Daredevil and the Kingpin make deals and work together. For instance, at one point, the Kingpin gave Daredevil all his files on all the crime bosses in New York—and Daredevil turned the files over to the authorities. Was the Kingpin going soft in the head? No way. He just wanted his rivals put in jail so he'd have the whole territory to himself!

After that, Daredevil and the Kingpin made another deal. Daredevil found the Kingpin's wife, Vanessa, who had been kidnapped. He offered to return her to the Kingpin, and in exchange, the Kingpin had to agree to call off one of his plans to take over the government in New York City. Both the Kingpin and Daredevil kept their word and delivered on their promises. But it *realllly* made the Kingpin mad to have to do it!

Finally the Kingpin got a chance to get back at Daredevil. He found out Daredevil's true identity as Matthew Murdock, a young lawyer, and managed to ruin Murdock's life. Murdock lost all of his money, was framed for a crime he didn't commit, and even lost his right to practice law! Then the Kingpin beat Murdock, locked him in a car, and sent the car zooming to the bottom of a New York river. But Daredevil escaped and . . .

Will Daredevil and the Kingpin both live to fight another day? It seems entirely likely—but only time will tell!

DOCTOR DOOM

Now here's a really bad guy—one of the worst. He didn't even have to change his name to make him sound more evil. His *real* name is Victor von Doom!

Victor von Doom wants to rule the Earth and destroy his archrival, Reed Richards, who is really Mister Fantastic of the Fantastic Four. Also, in his spare time, Doctor Doom would like to bring his mother back from the dead.

™

To accomplish these goals, Doctor Doom uses a number of superhuman abilities. First of all, there's his superior knowledge of science, weapons, and robotics. He is one of the world's greatest geniuses when it comes to scientific invention and has created a nuclear-powered suit of armor for himself. The suit gives him superhuman strength, plus it has a built-in jet pack. Doom also has a number of powerful mental abilities.

One last thing about Doom: you'll probably never see him without his metal mask. Why not? Because his face is disfigured. The poor guy got a scar on his face in college, and he was so vain that he thought it ruined his looks. So he made a metal mask to wear to hide his scar. Unfortunately, he put the mask on before the metal was cool—and now his face really is a hideous, ugly mess.

MYSTERIO

What happens when a Hollywood special-effects expert and stuntman gets tired of working "behind the scenes" while other people grab all the fame and glory? The answer, in Quentin Beck's case, is that he turns to a life of crime.

Quentin Beck, alias Mysterio, is basically an ordinary human being with special talents and skills, who wants more recognition. To get it, Beck has set a goal: kill Spider-Man! Beck figures that his own abilities as a stuntman make him every bit as good as Spider-Man, and he wants to prove it. He even created a Spider-Man look-alike costume and wore it while committing many crimes. (Boy, did that make Spidey look bad!)

But Beck's own costume and identity are as Mysterio. In his Mysterio guise, Beck wears a "fishbowl" helmet with one-way glass. It allows him to see out, while no one can see his face. He also wears gloves which shoot out various kinds of gas and fog. Some of these gases are simply used for effect—for flashy entrances and exits. Others are toxic and able to dull a person's senses.

Over the years, Beck has joined forces with many of Spider-Man's enemies, including the Vulture, Doctor Octopus, the Sandman, Electro, and Kraven the Hunter. Together they formed a group called the Sinister Six. After nearly every attempt to destroy Spider-Man, Mysterio has been arrested and thrown in jail. However he keeps getting out. So Spidey had better stay on his toes.

ELECTRO

At one time, Electro was a power-company worker handling the high-voltage lines. One day he was struck by lightning, but he didn't die. Instead, his body was transformed into a permanent source of electric power. Electro decided to use his new-found powers for robbery, blackmail, and revenge. He has always been stopped, however, and sent to prison, most often by Spider-Man. Electro's other crime-fighting enemies include Daredevil, Captain America, and the Fantastic Four.

Electro has so much current running through him that it is impossible to harm or kill him with electricity. If an ordinary person touches him, however, that person could be electrocuted. Of course, Electro gets a charge out of zapping his victims with a simple little bolt of lightning from his fingertips.

VULTURE

The Vulture is an old man and inventor named Adrian Toomes. For many years, he led a quiet life as an electronic engineer. But when his business partner cheated him, Toomes decided to get revenge. He invented a harness and set of wings that allowed him to fly like a bird. To his great pleasure and surprise, he discovered that the harness also gave him superhuman strength—superhuman for a guy his age, anyway.

Toomes enjoyed seeking revenge on his business partner so much that he embarked on a life of full time crime. He has repeatedly battled Spider-Man, been sent to jail when defeated, and then escaped from prison again.

MASTERMIND

Although Mastermind isn't a leader in the world of evil, he tries hard. He has done enough damage in his foul life to earn a spot among the Baddest Bad Guys around. Most often, he uses his powers against the X-Men.

Mastermind's main talent is that he can create visions and illusions that are totally convincing. Even if a victim knows that the illusion is just a trick of the mind, he will still treat the image as if it were real. Using this same ability, Mastermind can make himself seem invisible. Or he can cause people to think that they are hearing, smelling, tasting, or touching things that don't exist!

Currently, Mastermind's whereabouts are unknown ... but he will undoubtedly return.

●●●●●●●●●●●●●●●●●●●●●●●●●●●●●●●●●●●●●

GOLIATH

Check out his resume: this villain has worked for many of the most villainous criminals the world has known! The Swordsman, the Mandarin, the Red Skull, the Grim Reaper, Baron Heinrich Zemo, and the new Masters of Evil are just a few of Goliath's former partners in crime.

Goliath's real name is Erik Josten, and he got his first set of superhuman powers from an ionic ray machine invented by a Nazi criminal. But over the years, the powers began to fade. So Josten visited an evil scientist who had a secret strength formula. When Josten took the formula, it combined with the strength he had gotten from the ionic rays and made him stronger than ever. In fact, after taking the formula, Josten was able to will himself to increase in size—from his ordinary height of 6 feet to as tall as 60 feet. Of course, at full height, Josten also became much stronger. When he realized what his powers were, Josten decided to take the name Goliath.

Josten was in Los Angeles when he first developed his Goliath powers, and there he battled with the Avengers. For a while, he was held captive in the Avengers Compound on the West Coast. Later he was freed, but is currently in jail.

MOLE MAN

Short, fat, ugly, and almost blind—that's the Mole Man for you. Plus he wears a poorly fitting ugly green suit that makes him look like a nerdy elf. Plus he has bad posture!

If that sounds too weird to be dangerous, don't be fooled! The Mole Man is one of the all-time toughest little runts ever to tangle with the Avengers, Iron Man, the Hulk, the Fantastic Four, and the X-Men. And even though he has no superhuman powers himself, he has survived battles with all of those super heroes, on more than one occasion.

The Mole Man lives underground most of the time, in a world of dank caverns he calls Subterranea. Down there he's king, of course. But that's never been enough for the greedy little guy. So every now and then he surfaces and tries to either take over the Earth or destroy it—depending on his mood. One typical plan involved destroying all of Earth's power stations, and then setting free a bunch of monsters to destroy the human beings. Another plan involved blinding everyone on Earth with special ray devices.

Since he has no superhuman powers, you might wonder how the Mole Man manages to do so much damage. The answer is easy: he commands a horde of subterranean monsters, and he has great weapons, too. Mole Man has a whole set of staffs that look like ordinary wooden walking sticks or clubs. But each one secretly contains a different kind of weapon such as a flame-thrower or a laser cannon. No one knows what will come out of his stick the next time he appears on the scene!

Let's face it: the Mole Man wouldn't be a lot of fun at a picnic.

• •

LOKI

Talk about being jealous of your brother! Talk about throwing a tantrum! Talk about being ungrateful to the father who adopted you! Loki, the adopted brother of Thor, just about takes the prize in *all* of those categories.

First things first: Loki is the adopted son of Odin, lord of the gods of Asgard.

When young, Loki was called the "god of mischief," but lately he's earned the title "god of evil." Loki's basic problem is that he wants to take over as ruler of Asgard when Thor's father, Odin, dies or gives up the throne. But of course Thor is supposed to inherit that title. So Loki wants to destroy Thor, and he's willing to do just about anything to succeed.

27

Loki's main weapons are his abilities with magic and sorcery. He can give magical, superhuman powers to other beings. And he can change his own shape into that of another.

Physically, Loki has all the characteristics of an Asgardian god: he can lift about 30 tons, he is very long-lived, he is immune to disease, and he is resistant to injury. In other words, it's very unlikely that anyone will ever kill the guy. Instead, Thor is just going to have to keep beating him at his own game.

GOOD, BAD, OR IN BETWEEN?

THE PUNISHER

TM

Often, in the world of super heroes and powerful villains, the players change sides. Sometimes a good guy will be mentally controlled or tricked into joining an evil team.

Other times, a villain will suddenly get a conscience—and decide to use his powers for the good of humanity.

And some superhuman beings are so complex that it's hard to say whether they're good, bad, or in between.

Take the Punisher, for example. The Punisher is a vigilante who takes the law into his own hands. He uses a wide variety of lethal weapons, including an M16 automatic rifle, with which he has actually killed criminals. At one point, the Punisher even went crazy (after being drugged with a mind-altering chemical) and he began shooting at minor criminals—like litterbugs and traffic violators! For that reason, both Spider-Man and Daredevil disapprove of the Punisher's activities, even though he has sometimes aided Spider-Man against his foes.

But two of the most fascinating and confusing people in the Marvel Universe are the Hulk and Magneto. The Hulk is so violent, you can't call him a hero . . . yet so good at heart that you can't really hate him, either.

And then there's Magneto—a man who would belong in the Baddest Bad Guys chapter if it weren't for the fact that he has occasionally switched sides! Or has he????

Read the profiles below and find out what makes each of these strange people tick.

• •

HULK

Bruce Banner was a brilliant scientist who designed a nuclear bomb using gamma rays. Just as the bomb was about to be tested in the desert of New Mexico, a teenager named Rick Jones accidentally wandered into

TM

the test site. Bruce told another scientist to hold the count-down while he got the teenager out of there. But the other scientist was secretly an enemy agent, and he set off the bomb on purpose while Bruce Banner was on the field. The agent expected the bomb to kill Banner, but it didn't. Instead, the huge dose of gamma radiation turned him into the Hulk.

In the very early days, the Hulk only appeared at sunset and disappeared at dawn, kind of like a werewolf or vampire. Then later, the Hulk appeared when Bruce got excited, angry, or upset. As the Hulk, he didn't really remember being Bruce Banner, and he didn't have Bruce's intelligence. Consequently, he often destroyed people and property and was a total menace to society.

At certain times in his life, Bruce Banner has been able to control the Hulk, and he was even a member of the crime-fighting Avengers for awhile. But at other times, the Hulk has gone into such a destructive rage that nobody could control him! At times like that, he's been known to turn a perfectly lovely home into a pile of . . . well . . . gravel.

More recently, however, a scientist separated Bruce Banner's personality and body from the Hulk. So for a while, the Hulk and Bruce were two separate beings. Believing that he could now live a normal life—a mistaken idea, as it turned out—Bruce got married.

But then some more ugly changes began to happen. And here's the latest: Bruce seems to have a split personality. Sometimes he now turns into the green Hulk. But sometimes he turns into a *gray* Hulk, instead! And here's the scariest part: the new Hulks may not be so dumb. In fact, the two different Hulks, combined with Bruce Banner's personality, may be very smart and cunning as well. If so, that means the Hulk is one of the most powerful—and most dangerous—beings around.

· ·

MAGNETO

Magneto's life is shrouded in mystery—starting with his name and true identity. His real name is unknown, although he has used the name Magnus from time to time. His place of birth is also unknown. The only thing that is known about Magneto's early life is that he was a prisoner in Auschwitz, a Nazi concentration camp during World War II. Apparently, he had superhuman powers then but didn't realize it, or was unable to use them because he was suffering so much.

All of Magneto's family members died in the camps, but he survived. He then married and had some children, but when his wife found out that he had superhuman powers she was terrified and left him. After that, Magneto went to Israel, where he met Professor Xavier and helped Xavier defeat the leader of HYDRA, the evil Nazi group.

TM

After that, Professor X went his own way and started the X-Men. But Magneto took another path. He decided that mutants should take over and rule the human beings on Earth. (Of course, Magneto figured that he'd be the one in charge!)

By this time Magneto had full use of his powers. He is able to control magnetism and magnetic fields in so many ways that his power is virtually limitless! For instance, Magneto can lift a 30,000-ton object into the air, using the force of his mind alone! He can also put machines together in a matter of moments, using mental energy. And he can project all kinds of energy—like heat, light, or radio waves—from his fingertips or his mind!

In his quest to dominate the Earth, Magneto found himself repeatedly battling with the X-Men. He also hatched a plot to defeat all the major nations of the Earth by causing many earthquakes and volcanic eruptions. But in the last battle with the X-Men, Magneto injured Shadowcat, a young female member. He felt so bad about having hurt her that he decided right then and there to change his ways.

From that time on, Magneto worked with the X-Men. He then surrendered himself and agreed to be put on trial for all his past crimes. But the trial was disrupted, and Professor Xavier had to leave suddenly. So Xavier asked his old friend and enemy, Magneto, to take over the School for Gifted Youngsters. In other words, Xavier left Magneto in charge of the X-Men!

These days, however, Magneto is back to being a full-time villain, which doesn't surprise his old enemies one bit.

So is Magneto really good, bad, or in between? Only time will tell.

TOUGHEST TEAMS

When one super hero isn't enough—how about four? When four aren't enough, how about a whole gang of mutants with superhuman powers?

Even super heroes like company, which is why they've been teaming up for so many years. Here's a guide to some of the toughest teams of crime-fighters—*and* some of the most gruesome groups of bad guys the world has ever known!

•••

FANTASTIC FOUR

This was the first and still is the most respected team of super heroes anywhere, anytime, anyhow. The original Fantastic Four was started by Reed Richards, a supersmart scientist and billionaire who was determined to create a starship that could travel to other solar systems.

After spending most of his own money and government funds on the project, Richards' starship was ready to go. The pilot for the test flight was Ben Grimm, Reed's best friend from his college days. Reed was on board as well, and there were two passengers—Susan Storm, who was Reed's girlfriend at the time, and Susan's younger brother, Johnny.

But on the first test flight of the starship, something went wrong and the entire ship was bombarded with intense cosmic radiation. The four people on board all experienced changes that gave them super-human powers. Reed convinced them to band together and use their superhuman powers for the good of humanity. Reed named the team the Fantastic Four, and each team member chose his or her own name.

Reed, who discovered that he could stretch his body into any shape, decided to call himself Mister Fantastic. Reed's best friend, Ben Grimm, became a very strong but seriously ugly guy with thick, crusty orange scales. Ben Grimm was terribly upset by the hideous changes to his body, and so he named himself the Thing. Susan

TM

MR. FANTASTIC

36

Storm, Reed Richards' girlfriend and later his wife, found she could become invisible at will, and called herself the Invisible Woman. And lastly, Susan's younger brother, Johnny, took the name the Human Torch when he discovered that he could create a layer of fire around his body.

In recent years, the members of the Fantastic Four have sometimes taken off for a while. When that happens, a substitute member is admitted into the group. Among the newer members are the She-Hulk, Power Man, Crystal, and Medusa. Most recently, the old Fantastic Four disappeared completely and were replaced by a new group of super hero friends—Spider-Man, Wolverine, Ghost Rider, and the Incredible Hulk! But the original Fantastic Four will always remain the most important, and beloved, members of this fantastic, favorite super hero team.

THING

X-MEN

The people who form the X-Men are called mutants, which means that they were *born* with some kind of superhuman ability that other people don't have. That makes mutants different from many super heroes, who gained their superhuman powers later in life, through some sort of accidental radiation or other event.

The X-Men was founded by Professor Charles Xavier (but you can call him Professor X for short), who started a School for Gifted Youngsters in Westchester County, New York. Professor X's idea was that mutants should learn how to use their powers properly and be trained to fight against any other mutants who might intend to use their powers for criminal purposes. Consequently, the original X-Men were quite young when they were recruited by Professor Xavier, but they have since become adults.

Professor X himself is a mutant with tremendously strong mental powers, called *p s i o n i c* power or telepathic power. He

PROFESSOR X

TM

38

finds new members by sensing the psionic power in other people—sometimes before those people even know they have it!

Through the years, the X-Men have battled many evil forces, but their biggest foe has been Magneto. Magneto is a tricky, slippery dude who even managed to become the X-Men's leader for a short time! But now he's back to his evil ways.

Members of the X-Men come and go all the time. Sometimes they are injured or lose their powers. Other times they are tricked into betraying the team. And some of the original X-Men left the group to form their own group, called X-Factor (see below). Professor X is also the founder and leader of a group of young mutants called the New Mutants.

X-FACTOR

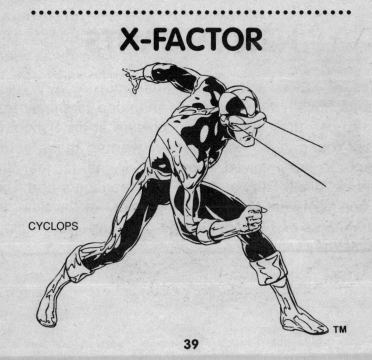

CYCLOPS

TM

Five of the most important members of the X-Men left that group in order to form their own group of mutants. The founding members of X-Factor are Cyclops (Scott Summers), Archangel, the Beast, the Iceman, and Marvel Girl, alias Jean Grey.

But here's the twist: at first, the members of X-Factor didn't want the public to know that they were mutants. So they *said* that their real purpose was to hunt down mutants and capture them! In truth, however, they were really trying to do the same thing Professor Xavier taught them to do, which is find other mutants and train them to use their powers properly. These days, the members of X-Factor have been more honest about their own identities and goals.

• •

NEW MUTANTS

Professor Xavier also started this group of very young mutants, mostly teenagers. He intended to simply train them to use their superhuman powers at his School for Gifted Youngsters. Xavier never wanted these young mutants to get involved in battling villains, for fear they would be killed. But you know how teenagers are! They just don't do what they're told! So most of the time, the New Mutants end up fighting the bad guys—and most of the time they win.

AVENGERS

Just about every well-known super hero has been a member of the Avengers at one time or another—even Spider-Man, who previously preferred to go it alone. Members come and go, or they take leaves of absence, so that altogether there have been dozens of members of the group. There are now two branches of this organization: the East Coast Avengers and the West Coast Avengers. The East Coast Avengers hang out in a mansion on Fifth Avenue in New York City, while the West Coast Avengers occupy a huge compound near the ocean.

The biggest difference between this group and the other superhuman teams is that the Avengers are known and approved by the U.S. government and the United Nations. They also work closely with the worldwide intelligence agency called SHIELD.

Thor, Iron Man, Ant-Man, the Wasp, and the Hulk were the founding members of the group. Here's a partial list of super heroes who have also become Avenger team members: Captain America, Hawkeye, Scarlet Witch, Vision, Black Widow, the Beast, Wonder Man, She-Hulk, Ms. Marvel, the Thing, Sub-Mariner, Henry Pym (in his many forms), and even Rick Jones—an honorary member who has no super powers whatsoever.

IRON MAN   TM

SHIELD

SHIELD is a worldwide peacekeeping and intelligence organization with members from all the nations of the world. It was started to counteract the evil activities of HYDRA. Its leader is Nick Fury. The initials in SHIELD stand for Strategic Hazard Intervention Espionage Logistics Directorate.

HYDRA

Major evil on a major level—that's HYDRA, a worldwide organization that was dedicated to dominating the Earth. It was founded by Baron Wolfgang von Strucker, a Nazi, during World War II, and at one time HYDRA was enormously powerful. The name HYDRA was chosen because it refers to a monster from Greek mythology—a many-headed creature that was able to grow two heads for every one that was cut off! In the same way, HYDRA always claimed that it would come back stronger than ever after any defeat.

SHIELD battled HYDRA on and off for many years, but finally Strucker was killed and the organization was weakened. However, after many years, Strucker came back from the dead and is now HYDRA's commander again!

SERPENT SOCIETY

An organization of criminals whose costumes and names are all based on snakes, this group has most often fought Captain America. Members include the leader, Sidewinder, plus Asp, Cobra, Cottonmouth, Diamondback, Death Adder, and others. These members hire themselves out to do "contract" jobs for other criminals. They can never be jailed—or not for long, anyway—because Sidewinder has a cloak which can "teleport" or mentally transport his friends from one place to another. Needless to say, they don't need vehicles!

TOP FIVE FEMALE CRIME-FIGHTERS

They're smart, they're strong, they're beautiful, and they're leaders! Here are five of the most fantastic female super heroes in the Marvel Universe.

······························

WASP

Like many other costumed crime-fighters, Janet van Dyne began her career after a tragedy: her father, a brilliant scientist, was murdered by an alien being. Janet became determined to avenge his death, so she

contacted another
scientific genius,
Henry Pym, and
asked for his help.

Henry Pym was
secretly the Ant-
Man at the time.
When he was
convinced that
Janet was sin-
cere about wanting
to fight crime, he im-
planted wasp cells in
her shoulders and
changed her into the
Wasp. As the Wasp,
she was able to shrink
to insect size, fly, and sting
her enemies. Later, Pym
also used his "Pym
particles" to give the Wasp
superhuman strength. Janet
eventually married Henry Pym, and for
many years they fought evildoers together. Later,
when Pym's personality changed, they were
divorced.

Together with Ant-Man, the Wasp was one of the five
original founders of the Avengers. For a while, she was
the chairwoman of the East Coast Avengers, but she now
works with the West Coast branch instead.

STORM

TM

Storm's real name is Ororo Munroe and she is the daughter of a long line of African witch-priestesses. She and all her ancestors have white hair, blue eyes, and magical abilities. In Storm's case, her superhuman power is the ability to control the weather. When her powers are intact, Storm can create or end storms of any size and throw thunderbolts from her fingers.

Professor Xavier met Storm in Africa and invited her to join the X-Men. For many years, she was a powerful member of the group and even became its leader. But then Storm's superhuman powers were accidentally removed when she was shot with a neutralizer gun. She continued as leader of the X-Men, however, and eventually her powers returned.

MARVEL GIRL / JEAN GREY

Jean Grey was the fifth person enrolled in Professor Xavier's School for Gifted Youngsters, making her the fifth original member of the X-Men. When she was a young girl, Professor X taught her how to use and control her telepathic and telekenetic powers. (She can make objects move, using only the force of her mind.) Eventually she took the name Marvel Girl.

Pretty soon, Jean Grey found herself falling in love with Cyclops, the leader of the X-Men, whose real name is Scott Summers—and they might have eventually gotten married. But a terrible thing happened to Jean. During an adventure in outer space, she was bombarded with radiation and almost died. For a long time, her fellow X-Men believed that a very powerful "Phoenix-force" had entered Jean's body after her death. The Phoenix had all of Jean's memories and Jean's personality, so the X-Men treated her as if she were really Jean.

In the end, however, the

TM

48

Phoenix turned out to be a separate being who was imitating Jean's personality. The Phoenix had saved Jean's life and sent her to the bottom of the ocean in a protective pod. There, Jean recovered from all of the radiation damage. Then she was revived and returned to the X-Men. Meanwhile, the Phoenix was experiencing severe personality problems, and she eventually killed herself.

When Jean was revived, the other four original X-Men decided to come out of retirement and form a new group. Now Jean, Cyclops, the Iceman, Archangel, and the Beast are all members of X-Factor.

SPIDER-WOMAN

With a name like Spider-Woman, she's got to be famous! In truth, there have been two crime-fighters calling themselves Spider-Woman—and both have had lots of attention from the media and the public.

The first Spider-Woman's real name was Jessica Drew. As a child, she was injected with blood from a spider that had been irradiated on purpose. As a result, Jessica developed great strength and immunity to all poisonous substances. She also had the ability to shoot off sparks. This was called Spider-Woman's "venom blast." For many years, Jessica lived as Spider-Woman— a private detective and crime-fighter. But eventually, in a very complicated series of events, she lost most of her superhuman powers.

The second Spider-Woman has superhuman powers similar to Spider-Man's. She can walk up walls, like Spidey, and she has superhuman strength which allows her to leap to great heights. Unlike Spider-Man, however, Spider-Woman does not need a mechanical web-shooter to create webs. She can create the webs using a mysterious mental energy. In the past, Spider-Woman worked for the U.S. government, but she also has friends among the Avengers.

Recently, however, Spider-Woman betrayed the government when she helped the Avengers escape imprisonment after they were wrongly accused of crimes. Then she fled and went into hiding for a long time. Now she is a full member of the West Coast Avengers.

SHE-HULK

Jennifer Walters, alias the She-Hulk, is about as smart, strong, and beautiful as a super hero can get while still having green skin. (Just for the record, she has green eyes, too.) And on top of that, she also has a great personality. Unlike the Hulk, she actually *likes* being transformed into a gigantic green superhuman. It puts her into a great mood. In fact, Jennifer would rather be the She-Hulk than an ordinary human being.

But first things first. How did Jennifer turn green, anyway? Well, Jennifer is the cousin of Bruce Banner, the original Hulk. (See page 30 for more details on the Hulk.) One day, Bruce came to visit Jennifer in Los Angeles, planning to tell her about his life as the Hulk. But during the visit, Jennifer was shot by some criminals. Bruce saw that Jennifer was losing so much blood that she might die. So he quickly gave her a blood transfusion, on the spot, using his own blood. It saved her life, but there was only one problem. Bruce's blood had been exposed to gamma radiation, and the radiation is what turned him into the Hulk. In Jennifer's body, the radiated blood had a similar effect. Bingo—green time!

As the She-Hulk, Jennifer is 6 feet 7 inches tall, weighs 640 pounds, and can lift 75 tons. She also enjoys life more when she's the She-Hulk, which is good thing since recently Jennifer was zapped with more radiation and now she can't change back to her human form.

For a while, Jennifer was an active member of the Avengers. Later, she was invited to join the Fantastic Four, to replace the Thing when he quit the group.

THE BIGGEST
BATTLE OF ALL TIME

™

Let's face it: when you put a dozen or more of the most invincible super heroes in one room . . . and then you put about the same number of criminals in another room . . . and then you zap both rooms into outer space and tell them to fight to the death . . . Well, it's bound to be the biggest battle of all time!

That's what happened when an incredibly powerful force called the Beyonder came to Earth to find out about "desire." The Beyonder was a force from the "Beyond-Realm"—another dimension. At first, he didn't even have a body. He was just a huge mass of power. But when the dimension opened and the Beyonder saw people on Earth, he began to be curious about them. He wanted to find out what made human beings tick—what they wanted and why they had desire.

So the Beyonder set a trap that would bring all the super heroes to Central Park in New York. Everyone came—Spider-Man, the Hulk, the Fantastic Four, members of the Avengers and the X-Men! Then he transported them in a huge circular building to outer space. He did the same thing with a great number of villains, including Doctor Doom, Doctor Octopus, Kang, the Lizard, the Mole Man, the Wrecker, the Wrecking Crew, and Galactus the planet-devourer.

When the heroes and criminals reached a place deep in space, the Beyonder completely destroyed a galaxy, just to demonstrate his power! Then he told them to slay their enemies and said that for whoever won the battle, "all you desire shall be yours."

The Beyonder created a planet on which the battle was to take place. It was called Battleworld, and the battles were called the "secret wars." The wars lasted for days, and for a while it seemed that Doctor Doom would win. Why? Because Doom somehow managed to steal the Beyonder's power—which was unlimited! But the Beyonder finally used another criminal's body and tricked Doctor Doom into giving some of the power back. (Smart move on the Beyonder's part.) It was touch and go there for a while and the super heroes were really sweating it! But once the Beyonder got his power back, he simply vanished. At the same time, he transported the super heroes and criminals back to Earth.

Before that, there had never been so many super heroes and villains in one battle—and since the Beyonder has since been destroyed, there may never be such a monumental battle again.

BEST WEAPONS

Don't look now, but someone named Oddball is sneaking up behind you. He's wearing a green, purple, and orange juggler's costume, with multicolored balls all over it. And he's about to throw one of the red balls right into your face!

Are you terrified?

No way! Get serious! Juggling balls as a deadly weapon? It could be cool . . . if Oddball didn't have such a totally nerdy costume! No, compared to Spider-Man's web-shooter or Wolverine's claws, a bunch of red and blue balls just don't make it in the world of high-tech weaponry. (Even if the balls *are* filled with poisons, acids, and explosives!)

Some weapons are cool . . . others are downright embarrassing!

Here is a list of the Best Weapons used by super heroes and villains throughout the Marvel Universe.

Spider-Man's Web-shooter

It consists of two metal cuffs, worn at the wrists. A steel prong extends down from each cuff into the palm of Spidey's hand. All he has to do to trigger the web-shooter is press a button on the prong. The web-shooter has a nozzle, called a spinneret—just like the spinneret on a real spider. The spinneret shoots out a web line in a thin stream, a thick stream, or a complex web pattern. If he wants to, Spidey can shoot his web a distance of 60 feet!

TM

Thor's Enchanted Hammer, Mjolnir

Made out of a mystical metal called uru, this hammer has several enchantments. It cannot be lifted by anyone who is not worthy. It always returns to the spot from which it was thrown. It can bring on a storm if the user stamps the handle twice upon the ground and wills a storm to appear. It opens the door to other worlds and other dimensions. And, in the past, it allowed Thor to travel through time but recently that power has been removed.

One of the best enchantments on the hammer, however, is the one that allows Thor to change into an Earth person named Eric Masterson. When Thor stamps the hammer once on the ground, he changes into a mortal human being, and the hammer changes into a walking cane. Eric can change back into his Thor form by stamping the cane on the ground again.

TM

The best thing about Thor's enchanted hammer is that he can throw it forward, grab on to the handle, and it will pull him through the air in a kind of flight. He can also "steer" the hammer, although no one's too sure how he manages that little trick!

••

Wolverine's Adamantium Claws

Wolverine doesn't know how he got them, but somehow he has claws. Real claws. *Razor-sharp* claws! They're made out of the artificial metal called Adamantium, and they're almost indestructible. They can also cut through just about anything! He has three claws on each hand, connected to his skeleton and nervous system. Wolverine can retract them at will, and when he does the

claws lie under the skin and muscles of his forearms. With claws like that, Wolverine is one cat you *don't* want to mess with!

Forge's Neutralizer Gun

This has to be the ultimate weapon: a gun that can take away a superhuman's powers! In the right hands, it could have totally eliminated all the bad guys the universe has ever known! Unfortunately, it was accidentally used against Storm, a member of the X-Men, and she lost her powers. Forge felt so guilty about this that he destroyed his neutralizer so it could never be used against a super hero again.

Hawkeye's Bows and Arrows

There are 36 arrows in Hawkeye's quiver. Twelve are standard arrowheads and six have three-blade heads. But the rest? Watch out! Each one of the remaining 18 arrows is a special-delivery surprise of one sort or another. One has a smoke bomb, another an acid tip that bursts on contact, a third is a 50-foot cable that unreels through the shaft. Then there's the tear-gas arrow, the rocket arrow, the putty arrow, the boomerang arrow—and even a sonic arrow that sends out a painfully loud sound two seconds after it is released! Needless to say, Hawkeye's victims get the *point*.

Daredevil's Billy Club

At first sight, it looks like a candidate for one of the *worst* weapons around. After all, how threatening is a blind man's cane? But that's what makes Daredevil's Billy Club so cool. His enemies don't know how dangerous that innocent-looking cane is! When Daredevil takes off the handle, it becomes a weighted fighting stick with deadly potential. It also has a built-in cable that Daredevil uses to swing from place to place. Together with Daredevil's own superb fighting skills, the Billy Club is a match for the best of them.

TM

WEIRDER THAN WEIRD

Cover your eyes. For that matter, cover your ears and don't let anyone read you a word of this! It's embarrassing, disheartening, and downright disgusting how weird some superhuman beings can be!

But if you must know . . . here are some of the strangest, most bizarre beings ever to populate the Marvel Universe. After reading this, you may look at the Thing and call him normal!

....

IMPOSSIBLE MAN AND IMPOSSIBLE WOMAN

First of all, they have green skin and pointy, bald, egg-shaped heads. Secondly, their costumes. Awful! Magenta turtleneck bathing suits! Third, check out their superhuman abilities. Sure, they can shape-change all they want. But guess what kinds of things they like to change into? A large number of flowers . . . a fountain pen . . . or a bag of water! Enough said.

PLANTMAN

This guy gets a "weird" award for his costume alone. He's trying to look menacing, but who can take him seriously with all those silly leaves hanging from his boots?

PUPPET MASTER

Not to make a big thing about it, but here's another bald guy. Most of the time, he's not really superhuman, but he has this special batch of clay, you see . . . and when he makes a clay puppet that looks like you, he can control your actions. Actually it's a pretty cool kind of power, but what kind of activity is this for a grown man? He ought to grow up and get a life.

ANGAR THE SCREAMER

He looks like a bad dude, he dresses like a heavy-duty biker, and here's what he does: he screams at you! That's right: Angar has the superhuman power to emit piercing screams—screams so loud that they cause the listener to have hallucinations! In other words, it makes you crazy. Oh, and by the way—he can scream for over an hour, nonstop!

OUTTA HERE!

When the going gets tough, the tough get going—on superpowered, superfantastic vehicles of course! Here's a comparison of some of the best ways to enter or leave the scene of a crime!

••••••••••••••••••••••••••••••••••••••

CAPTAIN AMERICA'S MOTORCYCLE

Details: It's a Harley-Davidson Custom Special which has been modified for him by a motorcycle mechanic. He takes the motorcycle with him in his van wherever he goes.

Top Speed—122 mph

Cruising Range—340 miles

CAPTAIN AMERICA'S VAN

Details: A custom-built Chevrolet with the following special features: bullet-resistant armor, security periscope, changeable side panel, satellite link for computer, hands-off steering, telephone synthesizer transceiver, acceleration-release device for motorcycle, exit ramp for motorcycle, automated first-aid dispenser, fold-down bunk with air mattress, music system, pantry, sink, and microwave oven. The gas tank holds 140 gallons.

Top Speed—400 mph

Cruising Range—4,200 miles

AVENGERS' QUINJET

Details: The Quinjet requires a crew of two and has optional seating for five passengers. It has vertical take-off and landing capability and can climb 7,900 feet in one minute.

Top Speed at Sea Level—Mach 2.1

Cruising Range—11,000 miles

SHIELD FLYING CAR

Details: SHIELD agents have use of the standard SHIELD Flying Car, of which there are about 2,000. In automotive mode, the wheels appear to be normal but for flight the wheels rotate out to a horizontal position. Special features include radar, a car body parachute, 30mm cannon and ammo box, gun camera, communications satellite, crew seat ejection, and armored hubcaps.

Top Speed at Sea Level—700 mph

Cruising Range—300 miles on ground, 550 miles in the air

X-MEN JET, THE BLACKBIRD

Details: Manufactured from Lockheed designs, in cooperation with SHIELD, the original Blackbird jet has been updated and modified by intelligent beings from another galaxy. Thus it is a unique aircraft. It holds a crew of three plus four passengers and contains escape systems and survival gear for a three-month period of time.

Top Speed at Sea Level—Mach 2.3

Top Speed at 120,000 feet—Mach 4.2

Cruising Range—12,600 miles

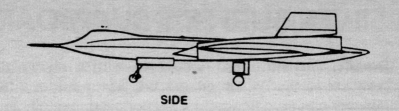

SIDE

TOP

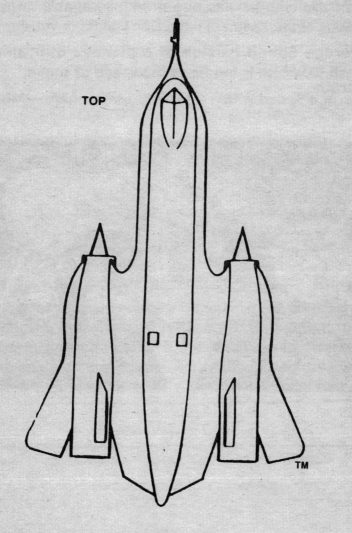

TM

67

SILVER SURFER'S SURFBOARD

Details: The surfboard is covered with a silvery glaze identical to that which covers the Silver Surfer's body. (Neither can be damaged.) It is controlled mentally by the Silver Surfer's psionic power and is capable of traveling at 99% of the speed of light! Don't blink, or you'll miss it.

Average Speed outside of a planet's atmosphere— Mach 10, which is ten times the speed of sound

Average Speed within a planet's atmosphere—Mach 5

TM

Q: Where do most super heroes get their costumes?

A: They usually make them themselves, the way Spidey did, or they are given the costume by a previous owner. For instance, when Anthony Stark, the first Iron Man, fell on hard times and wanted to quit his super hero job, he gave his Iron Man costume to James Rhodes. In Captain America's case, he was given his costume by the U.S. government—which explains why it has stars and stripes in red, white, and blue.

Q: Does Spider-Man have any weaknesses?

A: Yes, his spider-sense can be dulled by various gases, including the one Mysterio uses to dull an ordinary person's senses. Hobgoblin also has a gas that will do the same thing. Poor Spidey!

Q: Who is the largest being with superhuman powers?

A: It is Ego, the evil living planet, who is determined to conquer other areas of the universe. Ego is a planet-sized being with a diameter of 4,165 miles. Ego is also fully alive, with the ability to think, move, and . . . yes . . . eat! The planet has been known to consume and digest human beings!

Q: Who is the most unsuccessful super hero?

A: The most unsuccessful super hero is a ridiculous and pathetic creature named Frog-Man. Frog-Man's real name is Eugene Patilio, and he is the son of a highly unsuccessful inventor—a man whose only real invention was a set of electrically-powered leaping coils. When the coils are attached to boots, they allow a person to leap 60 feet into the air, or 100 feet forward. Eugene's father used the coils in his brief career as a costumed criminal named Leapfrog, but he was soon sent to jail. Then Eugene decided to wear the costume and become a super hero crime-fighter named Frog-Man, helping other super heroes such as Spider-Man and the Human Torch. As Frog-Man, Eugene is clumsy and has managed to defeat a criminal only once, accidentally. He also tried to join the Defenders but they wouldn't let him in.

Q: Are there any super hero twins?

A: Yes. Northstar and Aurora of Alpha Flight are criminal twins with superhuman powers. They are Andrea and Andreas Strucker, a brother and sister who call themselves Fenris. They must be physically in contact with each other in order to use their superhuman powers. When touching, Andrea can project a beam that destroys matter. Andreas can project a beam that feels like a superpowerful punch. Fenris often tangles with the X-Men and they have also had dealings with Magneto.

Q: Which of the martial arts does Daredevil use? Judo, karate, tai kwan do, or what?

A: Daredevil has studied American boxing and several of the Asian martial arts, and he uses moves from all of them in battle. His fighting style is completely his own— unique!

Q: Who was Captain America's partner and what happened to him?

A: For many years, Captain America had a teenaged boy partner named Bucky. Bucky had no superhuman powers, but he was brave and determined to help in Captain America's fight against the Nazis. He was killed (and Captain America fell into the English Channel) when a plane they were on exploded during World War II.

Q: Who is Rick Jones and why does he hang around with super heroes?

A: Rick Jones is the teenager who happened to be present when Bruce Banner was changed into the Hulk. Since Bruce Banner saved Rick's life, and since Rick was the only person who knew the Hulk's true identity, he became friends with the Hulk. However, when the Hulk became so wild and powerful that he was out of control, Rick Jones tried to help by sending a distress message to the Fantastic Four. The message was intercepted by other super heroes, and a very confusing battle took place. In the end, the Hulk joined with the other super heroes to form the Avengers. So Rick Jones became friends with them, too.

Later, when Captain America joined the Avengers, he took a special interest in Rick Jones. For a while Rick wanted to call himself Bucky—the name of Captain America's former teenage partner. But Captain America worried that Rick would not survive in the world of super-battles, and refused to let him remain as a permanent partner.

Through the years, Rick has had contact with many super villains and beings. Rick is still alive and seeking adventure with the many heroes he has known.

Q: **Which super hero has changed his identity many times?**

A: Henry Pym, a brilliant scientist and crime-fighter, has had five different identities. First he was the Ant-Man, a crime-fighter who could shrink to insect size. Then he decided to use his size-changing powers to grow bigger and gave himself the name Giant-Man. After that, he became the original Goliath. (There is another Goliath now—a man named Erik Josten who stole the name after he was treated with a stolen dose of "Pym particles.") Finally Henry Pym called himself Yellowjacket for a while. He is now simply Dr. Pym, an active member of the Avengers.

Q: **Do any of the super heroes have children? Are the children also superhuman beings?**

A: Yes, many of the superhumans and mutants have children and very often the children are powerful as well. For example, Legion is the son of Professor Xavier. Tattletale is the son of Reed Richards (Mister Fantastic) and Susan Storm (the Invisible Woman). Tattletale is still a very young child—in fact he's the youngest super hero alive today. But it is said that he has so much raw psionic (mental) power, he could destroy an entire planet!

Two of the X-Men—Cyclops and Havok—are the sons of a superhuman named Corsair. Now Cyclops has a son of his own, but it remains to be seen whether his son will be a mutant or not.

The most famous daughter of a superhuman is the Scarlet Witch, daughter of Magneto. Magneto also has a son named Quicksilver, who is the twin brother to the Scarlet Witch. Like their father, the twins have used their powers for both good and evil ends.

POWER GAME

Picture it: a world-class arm-wrestling competition—with all the best super heroes pitted against the roughest, toughest villains the world has ever known.

Spider-Man vs. Doctor Doom

Daredevil vs. the Kingpin

Captain America vs. Dragon Man

Wolverine vs. Mastermind

Who's going to win? Are the good guys really stronger than the villains? Is that why they always come out on top?

The truth is that for every super hero who can lift 50 tons, there's a bad guy who can do the same thing. But in the heat of battle, it often doesn't matter how strong you are. It's how well you use your weapons, your powers, and your *head* that counts!

Still, it's nice to know: who's got the power to pick up an entire gas station and hurl it 50 feet into the air? Who's stronger: the good guys or the bad? And which super hero is the greatest power player of all time?

So here's a list of the winners in the Power Game. Several of them—both heroes and villains—have what is called Class 100 strength. That means they can lift (or press) more than 100 tons!

....

HEROES AND VILLAINS WITH SUPERSTRENGTH

LEVEL OF STRENGTH

Hulk (when enraged)   **Class 100**

In fact, when the Hulk is enraged, his strength is almost limitless, which probably makes him the strongest super hero alive. When calm, he can still lift 70 tons. When the Hulk reverts to his human identity, Bruce Banner, his strength level becomes that of an average man who never exercises.

Thor   **Class 100**

When he wears his enchanted belt, Thor's strength is doubled, so that he can lift more than 200 tons.

Terminus   **Class 100**

Dragon Man   **Class 100**

Goliath   **Class 100**

Goliath has the ability to increase in size, growing from his normal 6 feet to as big as 60 feet. At 60 feet, he has Class 100 strength. At 6 feet tall, he can lift only 20-30 tons.

Wonder Man	**95 tons**
The Thing	**85 tons**
Sandman	**85 tons**
Iron Man (wearing armor)	**85 tons**
She-Hulk	**75 tons**
Loki	**30 tons**
Spider-Man	**10 tons**
Doctor Doom (with armored suit)	**2 tons**
Captain America	**800 lbs.**
Vulture (with his harness)	**700 lbs.**

The Vulture is an old, decrepit, bald man who ordinarily has no superhuman powers. However, when he puts on a special harness that allows him to fly, he also gains superhuman strength for a man his age, allowing him to lift up to 700 lbs.

Kingpin   **650 lbs.**

The Kingpin engages in intensive regular exercise and is as strong as any man his size could possibly be. All of his bulk comes from muscle, not fat.

HEROES AND VILLAINS WITH ORDINARY STRENGTH

The following super heroes and villains have the normal strength of a person their age, height, and build. Their physical abilities vary only by the amount of exercise they engage in. However, most of these people also have superhuman powers which allow them to handle a variety of life-or-death situations.

Punisher	**Intensive exercise**
Daredevil	**Intensive exercise**
Wolverine	**Intensive exercise**
Mister Fantastic	**Moderate exercise**
Human Torch	**Moderate exercise**
Invisible Woman	**Moderate exercise**
Professor X (world's most powerful telepath)	**Moderate exercise**
Magneto	**Moderate exercise**

Although Magneto has no superhuman strength in his body, he is able to lift and move enormous objects using the power of his mind. Once, he lifted something weighing 30,000 tons! If that doesn't equal Class 100 strength, nothing does!

Mastermind	**No exercise**
Diablo	**No exercise**

TEN MOST VALUABLE MARVEL COMICS

1. Marvel Comics #1   Value: $27,000

This 1939 comic is extremely rare. It introduced the Human Torch and Sub-Mariner.

2. Captain America #1   Value: $7,700

From 1941, this book was the introduction of Captain America.

3. Amazing Fantasy #15   Value: $4,500

From 1962, this comic contained the origin and first appearance of Marvel's most popular super hero, the amazing Spider-Man.

4. Amazing Spider-Man #1   Value: $3,900

With this 1963 issue, Spider-Man got his own magazine.

5. Fantastic Four #1   Value: $3,600

The 1961 introduction and origin of Marvel's first super hero team, plus the introduction of the Mole Man.

6. X-Men #1   Value $1,450

The origin of the X-Men was described in this issue, and Magneto was introduced.

7. Amazing Spider-Man #2   Value: $1,350

Included the introduction of the Vulture, one of Spidey's prime foes.

8. The Incredible Hulk #1   Value: $1,250

This 1962 comic introduced the Hulk.

9. Tales of Suspense #39   Value: $1,200

Origin and introduction of Iron Man.

10. Avengers #1   Value: $1,100

In this issue, the origin of the Avengers was revealed.